WITHDRAWN

Texas

AMERICAN

REGIONAL COOKING
LIBRARY
Culture, Tradition,
and History

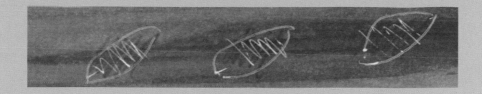

Texas

Mason Crest Publishers

Philadelphia

OTH
8/06

Mason Crest Publishers Inc.
370 Reed Road
Broomall, Pennsylvania 19008
(866) MCP-BOOK (toll free)
www.masoncrest.com

First printing
1 2 3 4 5 6 7 8 9 10

ISBN 1-59084-609-5 (series)

Library of Congress Cataloging-in-Publication Data

Libal, Joyce.
   Texas / by Joyce Libal.
       p. cm. — (American regional cooking library)
   Includes index.
   ISBN 1-59084-623-0
   1. Cookery, American—Southwestern style—Juvenile literature. 2. Cookery—
Texas—Juvenile literature. I. Title. II. Series.
   TX715.2.S69L53 2005
   641.59764—dc22
                                            2004006678
Compiled by Joyce Libal.
Recipes by Patricia Therrien.
Recipes tested and prepared by Bonni Phelps.
Produced by Harding House Publishing Services, Inc., Vestal, New York.
Interior design by Dianne Hodack.
Cover design by Michelle Bouch.
Printed and bound in the Hashemite Kingdom of Jordan.

Contents

Introduction
by the Culinary Institute of America

Cooking is a dynamic profession, one that presents some of the greatest challenges and offers some of the greatest rewards. Since 1946, the Culinary Institute of America has provided aspiring and seasoned foodservice professionals with the knowledge and skills needed to become leaders and innovators in this industry.

Here at the CIA, we teach our students the fundamental culinary techniques they need to build a sound foundation for their foodservice careers. There is always another level of perfection for them to achieve and another skill to master. Our rigorous curriculum provides them with a springboard to continued growth and success.

Food is far more than simply sustenance or the source of energy to fuel you and your family through life's daily regimen. It conjures memories throughout life, summoning up the smell, taste, and flavor of simpler times. Cooking is more than an art and a science; it provides family history. Food prepared with care epitomizes the love, devotion, and culinary delights that you offer to your friends and family.

A cuisine provides a way to express and establish customs—the way a food should taste and the flavors and aromas associated with that food. Cuisines are more than just a collection of ingredients, cooking utensils, and dishes from a geographic location; they are elements that are critical to establishing a culinary identity.

When you can accurately read a recipe, you can trace a variety of influences by observing which ingredients are selected and also by noting the technique that is used. If you research the historical origins of a recipe, you may find ingredients that traveled from East to West or from the New World to the Old. Traditional methods of cooking a dish may have changed with the times or to meet the special challenges.

The history of cooking illustrates the significance of innovation and the trading or sharing of ingredients and tools between societies. Although the various cooking vessels over the years have changed, the basic cooking methods have remained the same. Through adaptation, a recipe created years ago in a remote corner of the world could today be recognized by many throughout the globe.

When observing the customs of different societies, it becomes apparent that food brings people together. It is the common thread that we share and that we value. Regardless of the occasion, food is present to celebrate and to comfort. Through food we can experience other cultures and lands, learning the significance of particular ingredients and cooking techniques.

As you begin your journey through the culinary arts, keep in mind the power that food and cuisine holds. When passed from generation to generation, family heritage and traditions remain strong. Become familiar with the dishes your family has enjoyed through the years and play a role in keeping them alive. Don't be afraid to embellish recipes along the way – creativity is what cooking is all about.

Texas Culture, History, and Traditions

Think of Texas and certain images immediately come to mind: ranches and cowboys, horses and longhorn cattle, dusty plains and oil rigs. Now add NASA and the space shuttle, beaches and fishing along the gulf coast, rice and cotton farming, the Texas citrus industry, forests and highland lakes, mountains and cosmopolitan cities with tall office buildings, and you'll have a better idea of what Texas is like today. This is a huge state with four different geographical regions: the central plains, coastal plains, high plains, and mountains and basins. The state covers 267,000 square miles (691,526 square kilometers) and is a major agricultural area for the production of sorghum, rice, wheat, and dairy products. In fact, agriculture is the second largest industry in the state, and 130 million acres are devoted to it. The pecan is the official state tree, and pecan pie is a favorite in Texas. As you may expect, the state produces more cattle than any other state in the nation, but it is also the country's number one producer of spinach. Tomatoes, peppers, salsas, and sauces join with gulf seafood and Texas-grown fruits to create a more complicated cuisine than you may have imagined. But chili and barbecue are an important part of the history and food culture.

Campfires and barbecue pits still call to mind all manner of chili, beans, and barbecued beef. But Texas is filled with innovative cooks, and many foods are now barbecued in addition to beef—vegetables, fish, even pizza! Fried catfish and countless stews are also foods that can be made over an open flame. The long Texas coastline is sometimes referred to as the "third coast." If you're in a restaurant along the coast or in one of Texas' large metropolitan areas, you can order many delicious seafood dishes along with countless other types of food. The food history and culture of Texas are extremely diverse, but the emphasis in this book is on the more traditional foods.

Texas comes from the word *tejas*, which is the Spanish spelling of *taysha*, a Caddo Indian word that means "friend and ally." Pineda, a Spanish explorer, made a map of the Texas coast in 1519, marking the start of Spanish rule. When the Spanish explorers arrived in northeast Texas, Caddo people were already living there. The Spaniards in North America in the 1600s called the western part of the land inhabited by the Caddo "the great kingdom of Tejas," this is the origin of the state's name.

The state flag of Texas, the "Lone Star State."

The first Spanish mission was built in 1682 near present-day El Paso. When the Mexican government gained independence from Spain in 1821, the Mexican government gave Stephen F. Austin permission to establish a settlement of three hundred families in southeast Texas. Although they were not the first Europeans to settle in Texas, the "Old Three Hundred," as the colony came to be known, marked the official start of the colonization of Texas.

By 1836, the year in which Texas declared its independence, approximately 36,000 settlers were living there. Although Austin had a friendly relationship with the Mexican government in the beginning, tensions had begun to build, and several important battles ensued. The famous Battle of the Alamo marked a victory for the Mexican army, which still numbered upwards of four thousand after their last charge. After the battle, Jim Bowie, Davy Crockett, and William Travis lay among the dead; less than two hundred Americans had managed to fight off thousands of Mexicans for almost two weeks. Approximately six weeks later, Mexican fighters were defeated by General Sam Houston's army, which numbered half its size, at the Battle of San Jacinto. After this decisive battle, Texas gained its independence and Sam Houston was elected president. Texas became the twenty-eighth state in 1845. The Mexican influence, however, continues to be tasted in many Texan foods.

Before you cook ...

If you haven't done much cooking before, you may find recipe books a little confusing. Certain words and terms can seem unfamiliar. You may find the measurements difficult to understand. What appears to be an easy or familiar dish may contain ingredients you've never heard of before. You might not understand what utensil the recipe calls for you to use, or you might not be sure what the recipe is asking you to do.

Reading the pages in this section before you get started may help you understand the directions better so that your cooking goes more smoothly. You can also refer back to these pages whenever you run into questions.

Safety Tips

Cooking involves handling very hot and very sharp objects, so being careful is common sense. What's more, you want to be certain that anything you plan on putting in your mouth is safe to eat. If you follow these easy tips, you should find that cooking can be both fun and safe.

Dallas, Texas

Before you cook ...

- Always wash your hands before and after handling food. This is particularly important after you handle raw meats, poultry, and eggs, as bacteria called salmonella can live on these uncooked foods. You can't see or smell salmonella, but these germs can make you or anyone who swallows them very sick.
- Make a habit of using potholders or oven mitts whenever you handle pots and pans from the oven or microwave.
- Always set pots, pans, and knives with their handles away from counter edges. This way you won't risk catching your sleeves on them—and any younger children in the house won't be in danger of grabbing something hot or sharp.
- Don't leave perishable food sitting out of the refrigerator for more than an hour or two.
- Wash all raw fruits and vegetables to remove dirt and chemicals.
- Use a cutting board when chopping vegetables or fruit, and always cut away from yourself.
- Don't overheat grease or oil—but if grease or oil does catch fire, don't try to extinguish the flames with water. Instead, throw baking soda or salt on the fire to put it out. Turn all stove burners off.
- If you burn yourself, immediately put the burn under cold water, as this will prevent the burn from becoming more painful.
- Never put metal dishes or utensils in the microwave. Use only microwave-proof dishes.
- Wash cutting boards and knives thoroughly after cutting meat, fish or poultry — especially when raw and before using the same tools to prepare other foods such as vegetables and cheese. This will prevent the spread of bacteria such as salmonella.
- Keep your hands away from any moving parts of appliances, such as mixers.
- Unplug any appliance, such as a mixer, blender, or food processor before assembling for use or disassembling after use.

Metric Conversion Table

Most cooks in the United States use measuring containers based on an eight-ounce cup, a teaspoon, and a tablespoon. Meanwhile, cooks in Canada and Europe are more apt to use metric measurements. The recipes in this book use cups, teaspoons, and tablespoons—but you can convert these measurements to metric by using the table below.

Temperature

To convert Fahrenheit degrees to Celsius, subtract 32 and multiply by .56.

212°F = 100°C
(this is the boiling point of water)
250°F = 110°C
275°F = 135°C
300°F = 150°C
325°F = 160°C
350°F = 180°C
375°F = 190°C
400°F = 200°C

Liquid Measurements

1 teaspoon = 5 milliliters
1 tablespoon = 15 milliliters
1 fluid ounce = 30 milliliters
1 cup = 240 milliliters
1 pint = 480 milliliters
1 quart = 0.95 liters
1 gallon = 3.8 liters

Measurements of Mass or Weight
1 ounce = 28 grams
8 ounces = 227 grams
1 pound (16 ounces) = 0.45 kilograms
2.2 pounds = 1 kilogram

Measurements of Length
¼ inch = 0.6 centimeters
½ inch = 1.25 centimeters
1 inch = 2.5 centimeters

Pan Sizes

Baking pans are usually made in standard sizes. The pans used in the United States are roughly equivalent to the following metric pans:

9-inch cake pan = 23-centimeter pan
11x7-inch baking pan = 28x18-centimeter baking pan
13x9-inch baking pan = 32.5x23-centimeter baking pan
9x5-inch loaf pan = 23x13-centimeter loaf pan
2-quart casserole = 2-liter casserole

Useful Tools, Utensils, Dishes

barbecue skewers

basting brush

candy thermometer

cast iron skillet

cheese shredder

slow cooker

Dutch oven

flour sifter

hand juicer

pepper mill

stock pot

garlic press

wire whisk

Cooking Glossary

cut Mix solid shortening or butter into flour, usually by using a pastry blender or two knives and making short, chopping strokes until the mixture looks like small pellets.

dash Just a couple of drops or quick shakes.

diced Cut into small cubes or pieces.

dollop A small mound, about 1 or 2 tablespoons.

dredge To coat meat or seafood with flour or crumbs usually by dragging or tossing.

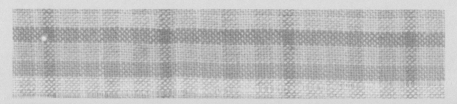

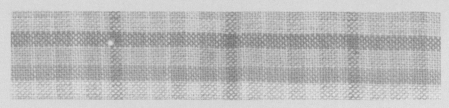

fillets Thin strips of boneless fish or meat.

marinate Allow a food to steep in a brine or other liquid in order to enrich its flavor.

minced Cut into very small pieces.

sauté Fry in a skillet or wok over high heat while stirring.

simmer Gently boil so that the surface of the liquid just ripples.

toss Turn food over quickly and lightly so that it is evenly covered with a liquid or powder.

whisk Stir briskly with a wire whisk.

zest A piece of the peel of lemon, lime, or orange that has been grated.

Special Texas Flavors

cayenne

cilantro

chilies

chili powder

cumin

garlic

salsa

Texas Recipes

Cornbread

Preheat oven to 375° Fahrenheit.

Ingredients:

1 cup flour
¾ cup cornmeal
¼ cup sugar
3 teaspoons baking powder
1 teaspoon salt
2 eggs
1 cup milk
¼ cup cooking oil

Cooking utensils you'll need:
2 mixing bowls
measuring cups
measuring spoons
wire whisk
9-inch square baking pan or cast iron skillet

Directions:

Grease the baking pan or skillet, and set it aside. Stir the flour, cornmeal, sugar, baking powder, and salt together in one mixing bowl. *Whisk* the eggs and milk in the second bowl, then dump it into the dry mixture, and stir just until moistened. Mix in the oil. Pour the mixture into the baking pan or skillet, and bake for between 20 and 30 minutes. (The exact time can vary from oven to oven.)

Tips:

Unless a recipe specifies otherwise, always use large eggs when cooking or baking.

Wooden spoons work well to stir batters.

Texas Food History

Native people in Texas have been cultivating corn for at least two thousand years. Scientists believe corn evolved from wild grains that cross-pollinated by chance some 10,000 years ago.

Corn originated in Mexico, where the Native people considered it to be a gift from the gods. According to Mayan and Aztec myths, the gods molded humans from corn dough. To ensure a good harvest, ancient people did whatever they believed necessary to keep their gods happy, strong, and generous so their crops would grow. Cornbread has become a tradition throughout the south.

Texas Food History

A hundred years ago, biscuits like these would have been cooked over campfires in cast-iron skillets. They would have provided a filling dish for hungry cowboys out on the range.

After the Civil War, a great number of horses and cattle ran free across Texas. These descendants of animals introduced by the Spanish explorers were available to anyone who could catch them. Texas already had a strong cowboy culture by that time, with African American and Anglo cowboys and Mexican *vaqueros* in the state. Many food traditions have grown up around that culture.

Cheddar–Sausage Biscuits

Preheat oven to 425° Fahrenheit.

Ingredients:

1 pound bulk pork sausage
1 minced onion
one 11-ounce can cheddar cheese soup
½ cup water
3 cups baking mix (Bisquick® is one brand)

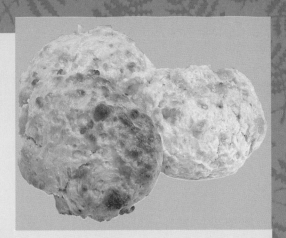

Cooking utensils you'll need:
skillet
measuring cups
mixing bowl
cookie sheet

Directions:

Cook sausage and onion over low heat until browned. Put the mixture on paper towels to drain off some of the fat.

Lightly grease the cookie sheet. Mix the soup and water in the mixing bowl. Stir in the baking mix, and then add the sausage. Drop the batter into little mounds on the cookie sheet. Bake until lightly browned (usually about 15 minutes).

Tip:

If you don't have Bisquick or another commercially prepared baking mix, you can make your own for this recipe. Just mix the following ingredients together: 2½ cups flour, 4 teaspoons baking powder, 2 tablespoons sugar, and ½ teaspoon salt. *Cut* in 5 tablespoons shortening, and then use this mix to follow the recipe above.

Corn Scramble

Serve this as a side dish for breakfast, lunch, or dinner.

Ingredients

4 slices bacon
1 small onion, chopped
1 medium sweet red or green pepper,
 chopped
4 eggs
one 15-ounce can cream-style corn
salt and pepper to taste

Cooking utensils you'll need:
mixing bowl
wire whisk
skillet

Directions:

Cook bacon in the skillet until crisp, drain on paper towels to remove some of the fat. Discard all but 3 tablespoons of the bacon drippings. Cook onions and peppers in the reserved drippings until tender, stirring occasionally. Add the corn and heat through. *Whisk* the eggs. When the corn mixture begins to bubble, stir the eggs into the skillet. Continue cooking, stirring occasionally, until the eggs are cooked through but still moist. Add salt and pepper to taste, and top each serving with crumbled bacon.

Texas Food History

When Spanish explorers arrived in the area that would come to be known as Texas, American Indians were already living there and growing corn. The new arrivals eagerly accepted it into their diet. Corn could be eaten fresh or dried, and could also be ground into cornmeal, making it possible to eat it at any time of the year. The taste, easy storage, and versatility of the food all contributed to its popularity. Corn was eaten in many forms and for any meal. Cornmeal could be made into a "mush" for cereal, into bread and pancakes, or into tortillas. *Masa* is a type of cornmeal that is made out of hominy, which is made with dried corn that has been soaked in limewater (water containing calcium carbonate or calcium sulfate).

Corn Chip Pie

Serve as either an appetizer or a main dish.

Preheat oven to 350° Fahrenheit.

Ingredients:

3 cups corn chips
¾ cup chopped onion
1 cup shredded cheddar cheese
2½ cups chili (canned or made with any favorite recipe)

Cooking utensils you'll need:
cheese shredder
measuring cups
9-inch square baking dish

Directions:

Put 2 cups of the corn chips into the baking dish and layer on half of the onions. Put half of the cheese on top of that, and pour the chili over it. Put the remainder of the corn chips on top of the chili, add the remaining onion, and top it all off with the remaining cheese. Bake for 20 minutes and serve hot.

Texas Food History

In 1932, Elmer Doolin, a resident of San Antonio, Texas, was waiting for his lunch in a local café when he saw a 5-cent package of corn chips on the counter. He decided to buy it to eat with his sandwich. The tasty chips were made from corn masa (see page 25.) Later when he met the maker, Mr. Doolin decided to purchase the business. For an investment of only $100 he acquired the recipe, a converted old potato ricer to make the chips, and 19 clients to purchase the product. Soon Mr. Doolin was making Fritos® corn chips in his mother's kitchen each night and selling them during the day. Sales were approximately $8 to $10 per day at first, and the daily profit was about $2. Within a year, production methods were improved and the company moved to Dallas. In 1945, H.W. Lay & Company became one of the first franchises for Fritos® corn chips, and eventually the companies merged.

Slow Cooker Chili

There's a great debate among Texans about whether or not beans should ever be added to chili. This recipe is for a bean variety.

Ingredients:

1 pound beef round steak
2 tablespoons chili powder
1½ tablespoons cumin
½ teaspoon celery salt
3 garlic cloves
1 medium onion, chopped
two 15-ounce cans kidney beans
two 15-ounce cans black beans
one 7-ounce can diced green chilies
one 14½-ounce can diced tomatoes, undrained
two 6-ounce cans tomato paste

Cooking utensils you'll need:
measuring spoons
garlic press
slow cooker

Directions:

Wash the meat, and pat it dry with paper towels. Remove any bones, trim off the fat, and cut the beef into ½-inch cubes. Place the cubes in the crock pot. Stir in the chili powder, cumin, and celery salt. Press the garlic over the meat, and stir again. (If you don't have a garlic press, *mince* the garlic.) Drain and rinse the beans, and add them to the slow cooker along with the remaining ingredients. Stir, cover, and cook for 5 hours on the low setting.

Texas Food History

According to some records, chili was first made in about 1850 by cowboy cooks who pounded dried beef, chili peppers, salt, and pepper into a sort of dried "brick" that traveled well and could be reconstituted with water to make stew out on the trail. Another story says that the women in a group of sixteen families first made a sort of chili in the 1700s after moving from the Spanish Canary Islands to what is now San Antonio, Texas. Still others say that chili originated in Texas prisons in the later part of the nineteenth century as a means of feeding prisoners using very cheap ingredients. Perhaps it's just a "tall tale," but one Texas story says inmates enjoyed prison chili so much that upon release they often wrote in for the recipe! One thing's for certain, "chili joints" began appearing in Texas after the middle of the nineteenth century. Some people say these small enterprises played an important role during the depression since a bowl of chili could be purchased for very little money. Another important historical marker for Texas chili involves the "chili queens" of San Antonio. Several women began selling chili in various areas until the city confined them to one location called Haymarket Plaza. Mention of the "chili queens" appears in writings by O'Henry and Stephen Crane. San Antonio now holds an annual "Return of the Chili Queens Festival" during Memorial Day weekend. Texas chili was introduced to a national audience at the 1893 Columbian Exposition in Chicago. With such a rich history, it's no surprise that chili was named the state dish of Texas in 1977.

A Final Word About Texas Chili from Lyndon Johnson, 36th President of the United States.

"One of the first things I do when I get home to Texas is to have a bowl of red. There is simply nothing better."

Texas Food History

Cilantro, also known as Chinese parsley, is a member of the carrot family and is actually the stem of the coriander plant. The Spanish conquistadors introduced this plant to Mexico.

Native Americans were the first agriculturalists in Texas, and beans were one of the earliest staple foods that they grew. People have been eating dried beans for thousands of years—but where did beans come from?

Most of them probably developed in Asia, Africa, or the Middle Eastern countries. It is likely that nomadic people, the ancestors of American Indians, brought beans with them when they crossed Alaska's Bering Strait. Dry beans can last for a long time in storage. That's one of the reasons why they were so important to the Indians and European settlers. In fact, some of the dry beans that have been found in Egyptian tombs were still able to germinate and grow when tested during modern times!

Bean Dip

Cooking utensils you'll need:
measuring cups
measuring spoons
mixing bowl
garlic press
skillet

Ingredients:

1 pound lean ground beef
1 cup **minced** onion
1 garlic clove
2 teaspoons cooking oil
one 15-ounce can whole-kernel corn
one 15-ounce can black beans

one 15-ounce can black-eyed peas
one 15-ounce can pinto beans
one 16-ounce jar salsa with chipotle
one 16-ounce jar salsa with cilantro
2 tablespoons minced fresh cilantro
tortilla chips

Directions:

Cook the ground beef in the skillet over medium heat, stirring occasionally, until done. Drain off and discard the fat. Put the ground beef on paper towels to drain off some of the fat, and set it aside.

Drain and rinse the beans, put them in the mixing bowl, stir in the corn, and set it aside.

Put the vegetable oil in the skillet and add the onion. Use the garlic press to press the garlic onto the onion. (If you don't have a garlic press, mince the garlic.) Cook over medium heat until the onion is tender. Add the bean mixture and heat through. Add the beef. Stir in the salsas, and cook until the mixture is hot. Sprinkle cilantro on the top, and serve with the tortilla chips.

Tip:

Store fresh cilantro in a plastic bag in your refrigerator for up to one week.

Texas Food History

Mrs. F. G. Ventura won the Texas State Fair Chili Contest in 1952, and her recipe became the "Official State Fair of Texas Chili Recipe." She continued to win the contest for the next fifteen years. Today, hundreds of chili competitions are held annually in Texas and across America.

White Chili

Chili is nicknamed "red" by many Texas enthusiasts, but this recipe is for a white variety. Try this twist on traditional chili.

Ingredients:

1 tablespoon extra virgin olive oil
2 medium onions, chopped
2 garlic cloves
three 15½-ounce cans white beans
2 teaspoons cumin
1 teaspoon cayenne
two 4-ounce cans green chilies
2 pounds cooked chicken
2 cups chicken broth
sour cream
tortilla chips

Cooking utensils you'll need:
measuring cup
measuring spoons
garlic press
stock pot

Directions:

Put the olive oil in the stock pot. Add onions, and use the garlic press to press the garlic over the onions. (If you don't have a garlic press, *mince* the garlic.) Cook until the onions are just tender. Drain and rinse the beans, and add them to the onions. Stir in the cumin, cayenne, chilies, chicken, and chicken broth. Bring the chili to a gentle boil, and simmer for about 30 minutes. Top each serving with a dollop of sour cream, and serve tortilla chips on the side.

Beef 'n' Beans in a Bowl

Texas summers can be hot, and a slow cooker is one way for cooks to spend less time in the kitchen.

Ingredients:

6 slices bacon
1 pound lean ground beef
1 cup chopped onion
1 cup ketchup
½ cup water
¼ cup brown sugar, packed
3 tablespoons vinegar
⅛ teaspoon pepper
two 16-ounce cans baked beans
one 15-ounce can butter beans
one 15-ounce can kidney beans
2 cups shredded cheddar cheese
½ cup sliced green onion
tortilla chips or corn chips

Cooking utensils you'll need:
measuring cups
measuring spoons
skillet
slow cooker
cheese shredder

Directions:

Cook bacon in the skillet until crisp, and then put it on paper towels to drain off some of the fat. Discard the fat in the skillet, add the ground beef and onion, cook until the beef is browned, drain off and discard the fat.

Put the ketchup in the mixing bowl, and stir in the water, sugar, vinegar, and pepper.

Place the beef in the slow cooker, crumble the bacon onto it, and add the baked beans. Rinse and drain the remaining beans, and add them to the pot. Stir in the ketchup mixture, cover, and cook for 2 to 3 hours on the high setting.

Serve in individual bowls topped with shredded cheese and green onion. Serve chips on the side.

Tips:

When measuring brown sugar, always pack it firmly into the measuring cups or spoons.

This recipe can also be cooked on the low setting of the slow cooker for 4 to 6 hours.

Texas Food Facts

All beans are just plain good for you. That's a fact. First take a look at what they don't have. There's no sugar, fat, sodium, or cholesterol. Now take a look at what they do have. They're high in fiber, protein, and lots of vitamins and minerals. If you're making one of the great bean recipes in this book, while you're at it, rustle up a batch of cornbread because when you combine beans with corn or rice, you get a hefty dose of essential amino acids. The town of Malakoff, Texas serves cornbread and pinto beans each year at the annual Malakoff Cornbread Festival.

Vegetable Hash

Cooking utensils you'll need:
measuring cup
skillet

Ingredients:

3 slices bacon
1 large portobello mushroom
2 medium ears of fresh sweet corn
2 tablespoons cooking oil
1 cup peeled and **diced** white potato

1 cup peeled and diced sweet potato
1 sweet red pepper, diced
½ cup chopped green onions
1 small poblano pepper, diced
salt and pepper to taste

Directions:

Cook the bacon until crisp, discard pan drippings, and place bacon on paper towels to drain off some of the fat.

Grill the mushroom. (If you don't have access to a grill, place the mushroom on a broiler-safe pan, and broil until soft and lightly browned. Watch it carefully, as this should only take a couple of minutes.)

Carefully cut the corn off the cobs (see "Tips") and set it aside.

Place the oil and potatoes in the skillet over high heat, and *sauté* until the potatoes are golden brown. Add the peppers and green onions, and continue cooking for about 3 more minutes. Stir in the corn and mushrooms. Crumble the bacon into the vegetables. Continue cooking and stirring until everything is hot.

Tips:

To cut corn off the cob, hold it upright and steady with the stem side down. With a sharp knife in your other hand, slice downward, cutting off a few rows of corn kernels. Then go back and gently scrape that area of the cob to get more of the corn juice. Some people like to place the cob in the center tube of an angel-food cake pan so the cut kernels fall into the pan. You still need to hold the cob steady as you cut when using this method. If fresh corn is not available, use canned whole-kernel corn.

Texas Food History

When is a potato not a potato?

When it's a sweet potato. Even though they share a name, these two vegetables come from different families. The white potato is a member of the nightshade family, and the sweet potato is a member of the morning glory family. Both originated in Peru, however, and both are thousands of years old. Sweet potatoes spread across South America and into Mexico. It is not certain exactly how sweet potatoes spread from South America to the Caribbean, but we do know that once Spanish explorers came in contact with potatoes, they were taken aboard ships. Columbus and Magellen both referred to batatas in their journals. Although this is a word for sweet potato, it is probably the origin of the word "potato" that is used for both vegetables today. Sweet potatoes were a good crop to grow in the Southern United States because they enrich the soil, putting back some of the nutrients lost through the growing of cotton. African slaves often grew and cooked sweet potatoes. The Spanish took white potatoes to Europe in the sixteenth century, and later they traveled back across the Atlantic to North America. The word "yam" is sometimes used to distinguish between two types of sweet potatoes in the United States, but real yams are another food entirely and are not grown in the United States. True yams can grow up to seven feet long!

Corn and potatoes are important foods to many people of the world, and a vegetable disease or pest can bring great devastation to the local population. The people of Gilmore, Texas, were so grateful after the lifting of a quarantine on sweet potatoes in 1935, that they have been celebrating the vegetable ever since with an annual festival they call the "Yamboree."

Steak and Fruit Kabob Salad

Tender steak, sweet fruit, and crunchy salad is a perfect summer meal. Texas now boasts an important citrus industry. Located in the Rio Grande Valley, the industry brings a tropical flair to Texas cooking.

Ingredients:

1 pound beef sirloin steak
1 apple
1 orange
1 nectarine
½ cup lime juice
⅛ cup steak sauce (any variety)
2 teaspoons brown sugar, packed

*2 tablespoons seeded and **minced** jalapeno pepper*
1 large plum
2 tablespoons honey
1 teaspoon minced fresh cilantro
*⅛ teaspoon lime **zest***
8 cups mixed salad greens

Directions:

Pour ¼ cup of lime juice into the mixing bowl. Stir in the steak sauce, brown sugar, and 1 tablespoon of the jalapeno pepper.

Wash the fruit, but do not peel it. Cut the apple, orange, and nectarine into 8 slices each, and add them to the bowl.

Wash the meat, and pat it dry with paper towels. Cut the meat into 1-inch cubes, and add them to the bowl. *Marinate* in the refrigerator for 20 minutes.

Cut the plum into 8 pieces. Place the marinated meat and fruit and the plum pieces on the skewers alternating the meat with various fruits. Barbecue the kabobs over medium coals for about 12 minutes. Turn the skewers frequently so all sides cook evenly.

Put ¼ cup lime juice and the honey into a jar. Screw on the lid, and shake until well blended. Open the jar and add cilantro, lime zest, and 1 tablespoon jalapeno. Cover and shake again, pour the dressing on the salad greens, and toss well. Place greens on serving plates, and top with grilled steak and fruit.

Tips:

Handle fresh hot peppers carefully. Wash them, cut them open, and remove all of the seeds. Discard the seeds and stems. Do not put your hands near your eyes when working with any food, but be especially careful when working with hot peppers. Always wash your hands with soap and water after handling these vegetables.

If peppers are too hot for your taste and burn your mouth, don't immediately reach for a glass of water. This is a rare case were water spreads the fire. Instead, drink milk, and swish this soothing beverage around in your mouth before swallowing.

Texas Food History

Cattle have a long history in Texas culture and cuisine. The first ranches were established near the San Antonio River by Spanish missions in the 1700s. American Indians tended the cattle at that time. Texas Longhorns, the hardy and impressive cattle that most people associate with Texas, evolved from the wild cows that composed the first herds. Cowboys on horseback would "drive" cattle to markets outside of the state. A highly skilled group of twelve cowboys could manage a herd of more than two thousand. In 1995, the Texas State Legislature named the Texas Longhorn the official state animal. Countless beef dishes are popular in Texas.

Steak and Potato Grill

Texas is famous for its barbecues. This recipe proves you don't always need fancy ingredients to "flavor up" key foods.

Ingredients:

4 beef fillets or loin steaks (about 1½–inches thick)
2 tablespoons cooking oil
½ teaspoon cracked pepper
¼ teaspoon salt
½ teaspoon thyme
2 garlic cloves
4 medium potatoes
1 lime

Cooking utensils you'll need:
small mixing bowl
measuring spoons
pepper mill
garlic press
basting brush

Directions:

Wash the meat and pat it dry with paper towels. Mix the oil, pepper, salt, and thyme. Use the garlic press to press the garlic into the mixture. (If you don't have a garlic press, *mince* the garlic.) Brush the mixture onto both sides of the meat. Slice the potatoes, rub them with cooking oil, and sprinkle with a little salt and pepper. Put the meat and potatoes on the grill, cover, and cook over medium/hot coals for 6 minutes. Turn everything over and cook for another 6 minutes (or until the potatoes are soft and golden, and the meat is cooked to your liking). Cut the lime in quarters, and squeeze a section over each piece of meat before serving.

Barbecued Ribs

There's no question about it, when it comes to pork or beef barbecue, beef is king in Texas. You can choose your own favorite, and pair it with the sauce in this recipe. Either meat will be de-licious when roasted over a charcoal or wood fire.

Ingredients:

4 tablespoons butter
1 medium onion, chopped
5 garlic cloves
2 large tomatoes, chopped
one 6-ounce can tomato paste
⅓ teaspoon Tobasco sauce
2 teaspoons Worcestershire sauce
½ cup brown sugar
1 tablespoon Dijon mustard

½ cup red cooking wine
1 lemon
dash of salt and pepper
Cayenne pepper
4 pounds spareribs (pork or beef)
2 tablespoons extra virgin olive oil
¼ teaspoon salt
¼ teaspoon pepper

Directions:

Squeeze the juice out of the lemon, and set it aside. Melt the butter in the skillet over medium heat, and add the onion. Use the garlic press to press the garlic over the onion. (If you don't have a garlic press, *mince* the garlic.) Cook until the onion is translucent. Add tomatoes, tomato paste, Tobasco sauce, Worcestershire sauce, brown sugar, mustard, wine, lemon juice, and a dash of salt and pepper. Lower the heat, and simmer uncovered until the sauce thick-ens (about 30 minutes).

Wash the meat, and pat it dry with paper towels. Rub it with the oil, salt,

Barbecued Ribs (continued)

and pepper. When the coals are ready, either push them to the sides of the grill so the meat will not drip directly on them, or cover the grill surface with aluminum foil. Place the ribs in the center of the grill, flat-side-down, cover the grill, and open the vents for adequate air flow. It takes about 1½ hours to grill these ribs. Turn them every 15 minutes during the first hour of cooking. Brush the sauce on, and turn the meat every 10 minutes during the last 30 minutes of cooking time. Monitor the meat so that the sauce doesn't "flame up" during the cooking process. Build up the fire as necessary while cooking by adding more coals.

Texas Food History

Some say that Texas barbecue can be traced back to German and Czech immigrants who moved to central Texas during the second half of the nineteenth century. Even though many cultures were known to cook over open fires, German butchers may have begun hand rubbing seasonings into beef and cooking it over different types of hardwood fires placed in pits. Perhaps they were influenced by local American Indians when developing their "pit" barbecue. Benefits of this type of cooking are the concentrated heat that cooks the meat and the smokiness that is imparted to its flavor. There are countless types of barbecue in Texas, and there is a great debate regarding dry rubs versus wet rubs, sauces, and marinades. Most Texas barbecue is dry. If a sauce is served, it is usually served on the side. Texas can actually be divided into four regions when it comes to barbecue. Accordingly, Central Texas maintains the influence of early German and Czech butchers, and East Texas favors barbecue heavily influenced by African Americans. West Texas likes an open-pit barbecue of the type that took place on cattle ranches, and, not surprisingly, South Texas has barbecue heavily influenced by Hispanic people. (After all, this is the area where Tex-Mex cuisine evolved).

Roots and Chops

In the spirit of range cooks who made one-pot meals for cowboys on cattle drives, this recipe calls for stacking coals on the pot lid and placing the pot in the fire. If you and your family are on a camping trip, you might want to try this recipe—however, your meal will also be just as good if you bake it in the oven.

Ingredients:

two 10¼-ounce cans cream of
   mushroom soup
¾ cup water
½ teaspoon basil
6 pork chops (about 1-inch thick)
2 tablespoons flour
¼ teaspoon salt

¼ teaspoon pepper
2 tablespoons cooking oil
1 large onion, sliced thin
1 cup sliced carrots
2 medium potatoes, sliced thin
½ cup sliced mushrooms
1 large apple, cored and sliced

Directions:

Mix the condensed soup and ¾ cup water. Stir in the basil and set it aside. Wash the meat, and pat it dry with paper towels. Put the flour, salt, and pepper in the plastic bag and give it a shake. Pour the oil into the Dutch oven, and begin heating it over hot coals or medium/high heat on the kitchen stove. Shake each chop in the bag, and put it in the pan. Brown the chops on both sides, and then layer the vegetables on top of the chops in this order: onions, carrots, potatoes, and mushrooms. Top the stack with the apples, and pour the soup mixture over that. Cover, place about 25 hot coals on the cover, and put the pot on the fire for 10 minutes. Rotate the pot, and then the cover, about one third, and continue cooking for 10 more minutes. Repeat this process once more, and cook for 15 minutes. (This is a total of 35 minutes cooking time.)

Check to see if The "vittles" are ready. If cooking in the oven, it is not necessary to perform any rotation of the pot. Just preheat the oven to 350° Fahrenheit, bake for 40 minutes, and check for doneness.

Beef Stew with Homemade Dumplings

One-dish meals that could be cooked in a big pot over the campfire were a common food served to cowboys out on the range.

Ingredients:

1 pound beef chuck steak
¼ cup flour
2 tablespoons cooking oil
½ teaspoon salt
¼ teaspoon pepper
1 teaspoon thyme
1 bay leaf
3 cans beef broth

¼ cup red cooking wine (optional)
4 medium carrots
1 large onion
3 medium potatoes
2 stalks celery
2 cups baking mix (Bisquick is one brand)
⅔ cup milk
fresh parsley

Directions:

Wash meat, pat it dry with paper towels, and cut into 1-inch cubes. Put the flour in the bowl, add meat, and stir to coat. Put the oil in the Dutch oven, add the meat, and cook over high heat, stirring occasionally to brown all sides. Stir in the salt, pepper, thyme, and bay leaf. Add the beef broth and wine, stir again, bring to a boil over high heat, reduce heat, cover, and *simmer* for about 1 hour. Stir occasionally while cooking.

Peel and cut the vegetables into chunks (about 1-inch square). Stir them into the stew. Add enough water to just cover the vegetable and meat mixture, bring to a boil, reduce heat, cover, and simmer for another hour.

Wash and dry the mixing bowl, and then put the biscuit mix in it. Add milk and stir to moisten. Drop spoonfuls of the batter into the bubbling stew, stir once, cover, and cook 10 more minutes (until dumplings are cooked). Garnish each serving with parsley.

Tip:

If you don't have baking mix, make your own following the instructions in "Tips" on page 23, and use 2 cups of that mixture with the recipe above.

Chicken–Fried Steak

Although "chicken" appears in the title, it is not one of the ingredients. Here "chicken" refers to the cooking method, since chicken is often coated with a flour mixture and fried. The gravy in this recipe is excellent on mashed potatoes. Add a mixed-vegetable salad and your meal is complete.

Ingredients:

4 beef cubed steaks
1 cup plus 4 tablespoons flour
½ teaspoon salt
½ teaspoon pepper
1 egg
1 cup buttermilk
2 teaspoons dry mustard
1 teaspoon powdered chicken bouillon
vegetable oil
2½ cups whole milk

Cooking utensils you'll need:
measuring cups
measuring spoons
2 mixing bowls (see "Tips")
wire whisk
skillet
candy thermometer
long-handled slotted spoon
oven-safe dish

Directions:

Put 1 cup of flour in a mixing bowl, and stir in the salt and pepper. Whisk the egg, buttermilk, dry mustard, and dry bouillon in the second bowl. Wash the meat, and pat it dry with paper towels. Pour 2 inches of oil into the skillet, insert the thermometer, place over medium/high heat, and heat to 360° Fahrenheit. Dip each steak in the flour mixture, then in the egg mixture, then *dredge* it in the flour mixture a second time. Shake off the excess flour with each dipping. Use the long-handled spoon to carefully place each steak in the hot oil. Cook until golden brown on the bottom (usually about 5 minutes), turn the steaks over, and repeat. Drain on paper towels to remove some of the excess fat. Discard the paper towels, put the steaks on an oven-safe dish, and place in a warm oven (325° Fahrenheit).

Save 4 tablespoons of oil in the skillet, and discard the rest. Whisk the remaining 4 tablespoons of flour into the oil over medium heat. Add the milk, stirring constantly. Cook until the gravy thickens, add salt and pepper to taste, and serve with the meat.

Tips:

Instead of the mixing bowls, you can use 2 pie plates. Using a shallow plate may make it easier for you to dredge the meat. Another alternative is to put the flour mixture in a disposable plastic bag, and shake the meat in it.

Many recipes specify seasoning "to taste." Always use caution when tasting hot ingredients.

Texas Food History

This dish is a specialty in East Texas. Some people think the Texas classic was first made by German immigrants to the state. That's because of its similarity to wiener schnitzel, a traditional German dish made with veal.

Oven–Baked Beef Brisket

Preheat oven to 300° Fahrenheit.

Ingredients:

1 cup prepared barbecue sauce (any brand)
¼ cup Worcestershire sauce
¼ cup liquid smoke
1 tablespoon garlic powder
1 teaspoon celery salt
1 teaspoon lemon pepper
1 cup chopped onion
½ cup water
4 to 6 pound beef brisket

Cooking utensils you'll need:
paring knife
measuring cups
measuring spoons
9–inch square cake pan

Directions:

Pour the barbecue sauce into the baking dish, and stir in everything else except the meat. Wash the meat, and pat it dry with paper towels. Trim off any excess fat. Place the brisket in the baking dish, and turn it until all sides are coated with the sauce. Place aluminum foil over the meat, and seal it well along the edges of the pan. Place it in the oven, and bake for 5 to 6 hours (until the meat is cooked through and very tender). Remove it from the oven, and let stand for 10 minutes before slicing. Put the sauce in a bowl, and serve it with the meat.

Tip:

For the most tender slices of meat, cut across the grain.

Peanut Ice Cream

You don't need an ice cream freezer to make this tasty treat.

Ingredients:

2½ cups unsalted peanuts, coarsely chopped
6 eggs
1 cup brown sugar, packed
3 cups whole milk
⅔ cup creamy peanut butter
3 cups whipped cream or whipped topping
hot fudge sauce

Cooking utensils you'll need:
food processor or nut chopper
measuring cups
wire whisk
mixing bowl
large saucepan
candy thermometer

Directions:

Use the food processor or nut chopper to coarsely chop the peanuts, and set them aside. Whisk the eggs in the mixing bowl, add the brown sugar, whisk again, and set aside. Pour the milk into the saucepan, and place over medium heat. Cook, stirring occasionally, until hot. Gradually pour about ¼ cup of the hot milk into the eggs while whisking constantly. Add another cup of milk to the eggs in the same manner. Now gradually pour the egg mixture into the hot milk in the saucepan, whisking constantly. Put the candy thermometer in the saucepan, and continue to cook until the mixture reaches 160° Fahrenheit, stirring often. Remove the saucepan from the heat, stir in the peanut butter, and cool in the refrigerator. Stir in whipped cream. Serve with hot fudge sauce and sprinkle the remaining chopped peanuts on top.

Texas Food History

Peanuts, grown commercially in Texas, were first developed in South America and then taken to Africa. By the fifteenth century, Africans were grinding peanuts into stews (a precursor to peanut butter perhaps?). Africans carried peanuts to North America aboard slave ships. During the eighteenth century, peanuts were already an agricultural crop in the southern part of the United States. The peanut is not really a nut at all; instead it is a legume, like peas and beans. Peanuts grow underground, beneath a pretty green plant. There are many nicknames for this nutritious food, including goober, monkey nut, earth nut, and ground nut.

Texas Food Facts

With over a million trees in the state, peaches are the leading deciduous fruit crop in Texas. Weatherford, Texas, in Parker County, calls itself the Peach Capital of Texas and conducts an annual Peach Festival each July.

Peach Cobbler

Preheat oven to 350° Fahrenheit.

Ingredients:

¾ cups flour
2 cups sugar
2 teaspoons baking powder
dash of salt
¼ cup milk
½ cup butter or margarine
2 cups sliced peaches

Cooking utensils you'll need:
measuring cups
measuring spoons
flour sifter or wire-mesh strainer
mixing bowl
small saucepan
2-quart baking pan

Directions:

Sift the flour, 1 cup of the sugar, baking powder, and just a dash of salt into the mixing bowl.
Pour in the milk, and stir until just moistened.
Melt the butter in the saucepan, and pour it into the baking pan. Drop spoonfuls of the batter onto the butter, being careful to not mix the two together. Stir the remaining 1 cup of sugar into the peaches, and pour them over the batter. Bake for one hour, and serve warm or cold.

Tip:

Another easy way to melt butter is in a bowl in the microwave. If you decide to use margarine, select one of the newer heart-healthy varieties.

Texas Triple-Chocolate Mess

Ingredients:

1 box chocolate cake mix (any brand)
1 small box instant chocolate pudding (any brand)
4 eggs
1 pint sour cream
¼ cup cooking oil
1 cup water
1 (6 ounce) bag semi-sweet chocolate chips
vegetable cooking spray
vanilla ice cream

Cooking utensils you'll need:
measuring cups
mixing bowl
wire whisk
slow cooker

Directions:

Whisk the eggs in the mixing bowl, add the sour cream, oil, and water, and whisk again. Stir in the cake and pudding mixes, and then add the chocolate chips. Spray the inside of the slow cooker with vegetable spray, pour in the "mess" mix, cook for 6 to 8 hours on the low setting, and serve with vanilla ice cream.

Texas Sheet Cake

Yielding about three dozen servings, this dessert is perfect for a crowd. It's also very easy to make because it utilizes several convenience foods. So whip it up for your next large family gathering or for a bunch of your friends.

Preheat oven to 350° Fahrenheit.

Ingredients:

2 eggs
1 teaspoon almond extract
1 box Devil's Food cake mix
one 21-ounce can cherry pie filling
⅓ cup milk
1 cup sugar
5 tablespoons butter or margarine
1 cup semi-sweet chocolate chips

Cooking utensils you'll need:
measuring cups
measuring spoons
mixing bowl
wire whisk
jelly roll pan
saucepan

Directions:

Grease and lightly flour the jelly roll pan and set it aside. *Whisk* the eggs and almond extract in the mixing bowl. Stir in the Devil's Food cake mix and cherry pie filling, and beat well. Pour into the prepared pan, bake for 20 to 30 minutes. Pour the milk into the saucepan, and stir in the sugar. Add the butter, and bring the mixture to a boil, stirring constantly. Boil for 1 minute, remove from heat, and add the chocolate chips. Stir until the chips are dissolved and the frosting is smooth. Pour the frosting over the warm sheet cake.

Further Reading

Cox, Beverly and Martin Jacobs. *Spirit of the West: Cooking from Ranch House and Range*. New York: Stewart, Tabori & Chang, 1996.

Foster, Agnes and Agnes Polasek. *Cooking with Texas Grandmas*. Flagstaff, Arizona: Northland Publishing, 2000.

Helms, Katherine. *Merry Christmas from Texas: Recipes for the Season*. Kuttawa, Kentucky: McClanahan Publishing House, 1999.

McKee, Gwen. *Best of the Best from Texas: Selected Recipes from Texas' Favorite Cookbooks*. Brandon, Missouri: Quail Ridge Press, 2000.

Miller, Mark. *Coyote Café: Foods from the Great Southwest*. Berkeley, Calif.: Ten Speed Press, 2002.

Spears, Grady and Robb Walsh. *A Cowboy in the Kitchen: Recipes from Reata and West of the Pecos*. Berkeley, Calif.: Ten Speed Press, 1998.

Stuart, Caroline. *The Food of Texas*. Boston, Mass.: Periplus Editions (HK) Ltd., 2000.

Walsh, Robb. *Legends of Texas Barbecue Cook Book: Recipes and Recollections from the Pit Bosses*. San Francisco, Calif.: Chronicle Books LLC, 2002.

For More Information

Facts about Chilies
whatscookingamerica.net/chilepep.htm

History of American Foods
www.whatscookingamerica.net/History/HistoryIndex.htm

Kitchen Safety
www.premiersystems.com/recipes/kitchen-safety/cooking-safety.html

Texas Agricultural Profile
www.agclassroom.org/kids/stats/texas.pdf

Texas Beef Council
www.txbeef.org

Texas Recipes
www.texascooking.com/cookbook.htm

Texas History
www.theus50.com/texas/history.shtml

Publisher's note:
The Web sites listed on this page were active at the time of publication. The publisher is not responsible for Web sites that have changed their addresses or discontinued operation since the date of publication. The publisher will review and update the Web sites upon each reprint.

Index

Author:

In addition to writing, Joyce Libal has worked as an editor for a half dozen magazines, including a brief stint as recipe editor at *Vegetarian Gourmet*. Most of her experience as a cook, however, has been gained as the mother of three children and occasional surrogate mother to several children from different countries and cultures. She is an avid gardener and especially enjoys cooking with fresh herbs and vegetables and with the abundant fresh fruit that her husband grows in the family orchard.

Recipe Tester / Food Preparer:

Bonni Phelps owns How Sweet It Is Café in Vestal, New York. Her love of cooking and feeding large crowds comes from her grandmothers on both sides whom also took great pleasure in large family gatherings.

Consultant:

The Culinary Institute of America is considered the world's premier culinary college. It is a private, not-for-profit learning institution, dedicated to providing the world's best culinary education. Its campuses in New York and California provide learning environments that focus on excellence, leadership, professionalism, ethics, and respect for diversity. The institute embodies a passion for food with first-class cooking expertise.

Recipe Contributor:

Patricia Therrien has worked for several years with Harding House Publishing Service as a researcher and recipe consultant—but she has been experimenting with food and recipes for the past thirty years. Her expertise has enriched the lives of friends and family. Patty lives in western New York State with her family and numerous animals, including several horses, cats, and dogs.

Picture Credits